MW00799240

Hide-and-Seek Clothes

Kristin Eck

Published in 2004 by The Rosen Publishing Group, Inc.
29 East 21st Street, New York, NY 10010

Copyright © 2004 by The Rosen Publishing Group, Inc.

First Edition

Book Design: Kim Sonsky
Photo Credits: All photos by Maura B. McConnell.

Eck, Kristin
Hide-and-seek clothes / Kristin Eck.
p. cm. — (Hide-and-seek books)
Summary: Simple text and photographs identify items of clothing.
ISBN 1-4042-2705-9 (lib.)
1. Vocabulary—Juvenile literature   2. Clothing
and dress—Juvenile literature   [1. Clothing and dress]
I. Title   II. Series
PE1449.E26 2004   2003-012822
391—dc21

Manufactured in the United States of America

The Rosen Publishing Group's

PowerStart Press™
New York

Where is the raincoat?

Here is the raincoat!

Where are the pajamas?

Here are the pajamas!

Where are the mittens?

Here are the mittens!

There is a pair of slippers hiding in this picture. Can you find the slippers?

Words to Remember

mittens

pajamas

raincoat

slippers